Renaissance Music

for the Harp

by Deborah Friou

for non-pedal and pedal harp

This book is dedicated to my music teachers, most especially to my harp teacher, Kenneth Custance.

I would like to extend special thanks to Sylvia Woods for all of her support and assistance.

Companion CD
A companion CD, recorded by Deborah Friou, is available to go along with this book. The pieces are played in the same order as they appear in the book. They are played at a slower tempo with minimal rhythmic variation to assist the harp player in learning the tunes. The CD may be ordered from your harp music dealer or from Hal Leonard Online.

Revised Edition.

All arrangements by Deborah Friou.
Cover art and illustrations by Linda Friou.

First Edition 1985
Revised Edition 1993

ISBN 978-0-9628120-4-0

Introduction

This book contains a collection of dances and ayres from the Renaissance period, arranged for the harp. Most of the pieces were written in the 1500's and were originally intended for keyboard, lute, or voice. Many of them are found in more than one setting by several composers and were considered the popular music of the day, to be played and enjoyed at home by the amateur as well as by the professional musician.

In the 16th century, a vast amount of dance music was published. Drawn from these are the corrantos, almans, and voltas found in this book. They should be played with a feeling for the strong rhythmic pulse typical of dance music.

The alman has a moderate, stately, almost heavy style. The corranto and volta should convey a light touch and quick tempo. The bransle has a swaying feel in keeping with the dance.

The ayres are characterized by the beauty of the melodic line and should be played expressively and sensitively.

All of the arrangements can be played on folk harp. Some do have accidentals that require the use of sharping levers.

The names of the pieces, as well as their melodies, are evocative of images of another time, of castles, lords, and ladies: a time when making music was considered an essential part of a cultured person's life.

It is the purpose of this book to bring to the harpers and harpists of today the music of the Renaissance.

Contents

Lord Willoughby's Welcome Home

Expressively

melody by Dowland

arrangement by Deborah Friou

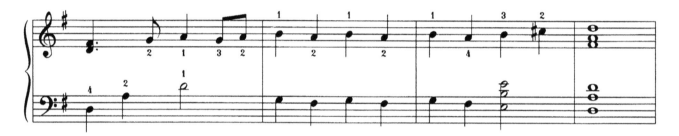

4

Corranto

Firmly

melody-Anon.

arrangement by Deborah Friou

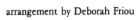

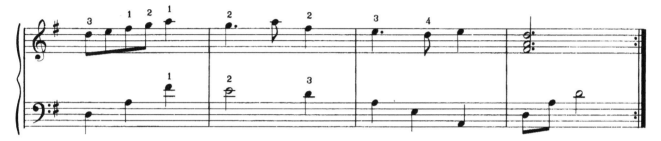

Toy

With Spirit

melody by Francis Cutting

arrangement by Deborah Friou

Bransle

Moderately

melody by Pierre Attaignant

arrangement by Deborah Friou

Corranto

melody-Anon.

arrangement by Deborah Friou

Lightly

8

All in a Garden Green

arrangement by Deborah Friou

melody by John Playford

Quickly

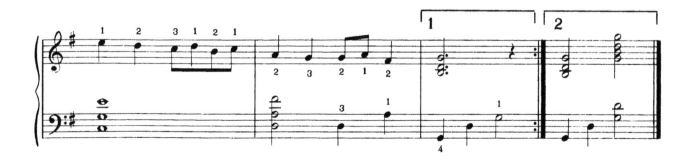

9

Nachtanz

melody by Tielman Susato

arrangement by Deborah Friou

Briskly

10 © 1985 by Deborah Friou

Alman

Moderately

melody by Thomas Morely

arrangement by Deborah Friou

Robin

melody by John Munday

arrangement by Deborah Friou

Flowing

Fortune

melody by William Byrd

arrangement by Deborah Friou

Slowly

Folk harpers sharp G above middle C

It Was a Lover and His Lass

melody by Thomas Morely

arrangement by Deborah Friou

Lightly

Folk harpers sharp the F below middle C.

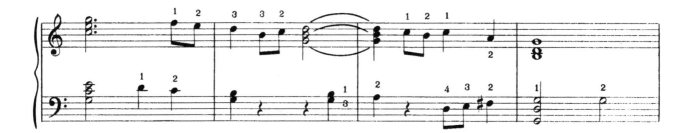

15

Alman

Moderately

melody-Anon.

arrangement by Deborah Friou

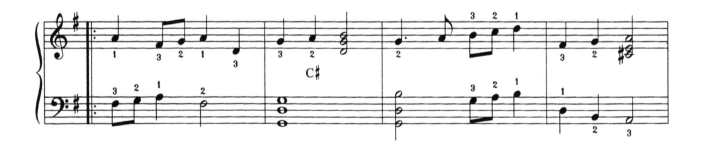

16

Corranto

melody-Anon.

arrangement by Deborah Friou

Moderately

Folk harpers sharp middle C and C above middle C.

Nobody's Gigge

melody by Giles Farnaby

arrangement by Deborah Friou

Firmly

18

Lady Riche

With Feeling

Lever changes indicated for folk harpers.

melody-Anon.

arrangement by Deborah Friou

Wolseys Wilde

melody by William Byrd

arrangement by Deborah Friou

Lively

La Volta

Quickly

melody by William Byrd

arrangement by Deborah Friou

22

Variation of La Volta

melody by William Byrd

arrangement by Deborah Friou

23

Greensleeves

melody by Francis Cutting

arrangement by   Deborah Friou

With Feeling

Folk harpers sharp the 2 F's above middle C.

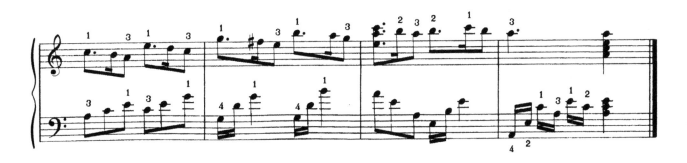

The Carman's Whistle

Lightly

Lever changes indicated for folk harpers.

melody by William Byrd

arrangement by Deborah Friou

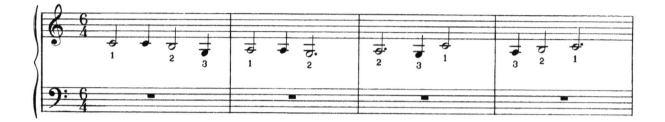

Variation of The Carman's Whistle

melody by William Byrd

arrangement by Deborah Friou

Hartes Ease

melody by Anthony Holborne

arrangement by Deborah Friou

Grandly

Lever changes indicated for folk harpers.

Folk harpers natural the F below low C

29

Alman

Stately

Folk harpers sharp the 2 G's above middle C. The high G will change.

melody-Anon.

arrangement by Deborah Friou

The Earl of Essex Galliard

melody by John Dowland

arrangement by Deborah Friou

Quickly